Preaching & Teaching

LAUDATO SI'

ON CARE FOR OUR COMMON HOME

Elizabeth-Anne Stewart

C. 2015

DEDICATION

To Diana, Patricia and Anne

For gracing my life

With so much love, support and encouragement

Despite the continents that separate us…

LAUDATO SI, MI SIGNORE...

Medieval Italian Praise be to You

Most High, all-powerful, all-good Lord,
All praise is Yours, all glory, honor and
blessings.
To You alone, Most High, do they belong;
no mortal lips are worthy to pronounce
Your Name.

We praise You, Lord, for all Your
creatures,
especially for Brother Sun,
who is the day through whom You give us
light.
And he is beautiful and radiant with great
splendor
of You Most High, he bears Your likeness.

We praise You, Lord, for Sister Moon and
the stars in the heavens; You have made
them bright, precious and fair.

We praise You, Lord, for Brothers
Wind and Air,
fair and stormy, all weather's moods,
by which You cherish all that You have
made.

~ 5 ~

We praise You, Lord, for Sister Water,
so useful, humble, precious and pure.

We praise You, Lord, for Brother Fire
through whom You light the night.
He is beautiful, playful, robust and strong.

We praise You, Lord, for Sister Earth
who sustains us
with her fruits, colored flowers
and herbs.

We praise You, Lord, for those who forgive,
who for love of You bear sickness and trial.
Blessed are those who endure in peace;
by You Most High, they will be crowned.

We praise You, Lord, for Sister Death,
from whom no-one living can escape.
Woe to those who die in their sins!
Blessed are those that she finds doing Your
Will.
No second death can do them harm.

We praise and bless You, Lord,
and give You thanks
and serve You in all humility.

St. Francis of Assisi, c.1225

CONTENTS

A PSALM OF GREENING

I

From the cosmic whirl
came light
from the dance of atoms
came light
from the swelling waters
came light
and darkness was overcome.
Greening things
filled the Earth,
creeping, climbing, spreading
over and upwards, spilling
blossoms of white and hectic red,
sun yellow and royal purple,
over hills, valleys, forests and plains.
Creatures crawled, swam,
slithered, leaped and flew,
bridling winds and waters,
taming rocks and sand,
homemakers in hollowed wood
and hallowed ground,
in rocky crevices
and the lofty limbs of pines.

And the Earth teemed, greening
under the blessing of the sun,
resounding with the songs
of countless choristers,
welcoming humankind
into a Garden of Delight
wide as the universe.

II

Eons later, here we stand
in this same Garden,
time shattered, now,
its freshness sullied,
soil bloodied,
resources squandered.
We stare at strip mines
and landfills, at dust clouds
and heaps of hazardous waste;
we hear the drone of bombers
dropping megatons of death
and smell decay
seething from the ground,
foaming in our wells,
blistering tender flesh.

III

O God, we are the stewards
of your creation,
caretakers of that greening power
running through the core
of all living things,
chroniclers of beauty, mystery,
and the ravaging of the Earth.
We know the fragility
of things past—
silence of extinct species,
stillness of dead waters,
flatness of felled forests,
haunting laments
of decimated peoples.
We fear the push-button ease
that can bring white
of eternal winter.

Give us a new greening, God.
Give us virescence
of aquamarine and emerald,
vegetable and olive,
berry and leaf.

Let green come
from the whirl
and the dance
and the swell
of *your* power
that chaos may be scourged,
all shadows dispelled.

Elizabeth-Anne Stewart. ***Woman Dreamer***,

INTRODUCTION

I have just returned from an art exhibition at the Bridgeport Art Center, Chicago, still numbed by the apocalyptic imagery in the paintings of Lelde Kalmite, a Latvian artist of some renown. I have followed Dr. Kalmite's work for several years now, for her depictions of conflagration capture the reality of life in the C21st: Earth is burning; all is spoiled and marred, the landscape charred. There is no life – only the fury of flames and clouds of toxic smoke that billow across canvas after canvas, a statement of where we already are and where we seem to be heading....

But apocalypse is not the final word. On my dining room table lies a printout of Pope Francis' encyclical, **Laudato Si'**, a document that unflinchingly names the crisis facing humanity while also providing spiritual solutions. My copy is already heavily underlined, and though reading it online would have spared a stack of seventy four pages, still, the hard copy allowed me to engage with the content at a deeper level than if I had merely scanned the text across my computer screen.

Personally, I find this encyclical both prophetic and comforting; it is "pro-life" in the ultimate sense, meaning that it holds that *all* life is sacred and worthy of our respect and careful stewardship. It invites us to celebrate the beauty of our "common home" and to behold, in awe and wonder, all that God has created for our enjoyment. While it is unflinching in calling humanity to account, ***Laudato Si'*** also gives us the hope that if we can only change our ways, the Doomsday Clock may lose momentum, perhaps even tick counter clock-wise!

But not everyone shares my enthusiasm. A host of politicians including Jeb Bush, Rick Santorum and Mark Rubio were quick to critique both the document and the Pope. On the campaign trail, Jeb Bush, a Catholic convert, made no secret of his dissent: "I don't get economic policy from my bishops or my cardinals, or from my Pope" the *New*

York Times quotes him as saying before the release of the encyclical.
(http://www.newsweek.com/jeb-bush-pope-youre-not-boss-me-343922)

For his part, Santorum thinks that "we probably are better off leaving science to the scientists, and focusing on what we're really good at, which is theology and morality." Of course, what Santorum neglects to say is that "Jorge Bergoglio earned a technician's degree in chemistry from a technical school in Buenos Aires before joining the seminary."
(http://www.motherjones.com/bluemarble/2015/06/dear-rick-santorum-pope-actually-did-study-science).

Writing for *The Remnant*, Chris Jackson claims that reading ***Laudato Si'*** amounted to nothing more than a waste of time and that, as a Catholic, he is embarrassed by the document:

> It is the Pope's latest verbose tome of an encyclical, which: espouses global warming alarmism, calls for international organizations to police

climate change, and waxes poetic about people leading animals to God.

I have to admit that I found Jackson's article to be a hilarious piece of writing with some equally funny graphics— like the one of Al Gore, the Pope's "ghost writer," breathing fire and brimstone on Planet Earth! Though I disagree entirely with this blogger's stand, I have to give him credit for a lively style. Take the following witty commentary:

> God created animals for man and not for their own sake. Thus, the ultimate purpose of other creatures is indeed to be found in us. Furthermore, we are in no way called to lead Fido, our pet fish, or dung beetles back to the Risen Christ. Our job on this Earth is to save our soul. Last I checked, Fido will not stand before the judgment seat of Christ to account for his life.
> (http://remnantnewspaper.com/web/index.php/fetzen-fliegen/item/1819-why-i-m-disregarding-laudato-si-and-you-should-too)

Here, I feel called to defend the humble dung beetle! According to the San Diego Zoo, dung beetles loosen and nurture the soil and control fly populations by burying excrement – in other words, they play a critical ecological role and help control disease. Jackson may pooh-pooh the existence of this creature, but, like Jackson himself, it does serve a Divine purpose! (http://kids.sandiegozoo.org/animals/insects/dung-beetle)

As for Fido, I very much hope he *will* be there in the afterlife, not to face the judgment seat but to enjoy his heavenly reward for being a faithful companion!

Contrary to the claims of global-warming naysayers, ***Laudato Si'*** is not a political document, nor does it settle scientific questions such as the safety of GMO technology. Rather, drawing on scriptural texts, Catholic teachings on social justice, Franciscan spirituality, objective data and the findings of science, ***Laudato Si'*** spells out the nature of this crisis and its roots in human choices. Simply put, we are facing an

genetically modified organism

ecological catastrophe of unimaginable proportions— and it does not just involve climate change! The document, in fact, points out the major ills that we humans have created through our greed, wastefulness, lack of vision and sense of entitlement— ills such as deforestation, the pollution of air and water, the extinction of species, the displacement of indigenous peoples, the contamination of the food chain, the loss of bio-diversity, the destruction of animal habitats, the acidification of the oceans, the proliferation of toxic waste dumps and so forth….

The list of problems is long and complex, and trying to comprehend this list "comprehensively" is beyond most people's capabilities. Even the countless scientists, writers, thinkers, artists and "ordinary people" who have, in their own way, exposed the scandalous reality of life on Planet Earth, tend to focus on a single issue. Al Gore's documentary, *An Inconvenient Truth* (2006), has helped enlighten audiences worldwide on the consequences of global warming, while Paul Hawken's *New York Times* bestseller, *Blessed Unrest* (2007), focuses on the global emergence of grass roots environmental organizations. Pioneers in raising ecological awareness include Rachel Carson whose *Silent Spring* (1962) awakened the public to the dangers of pesticides in general and of DDT in particular; Erin Brockovich who worked tirelessly to prove that Pacific Gas and Electric had contaminated the water supply of Hinkley, CA, with *hexavalent chromium*, a potent carcinogen; and Cesar Chavez, a Latino American civil rights activist who led boycotts of the grape industry in the 1980's to protest the widespread use of harmful pesticides and their effects on unprotected laborers.

The truth of the matter is that no one, including Pope Francis, can take on every cause— there are simply too many of them. What we *can* do, however, is become more aware of the problems and of *our* role in creating them. None of us, not even the most environmentally-conscious activist, is without guilt at some level. We all generate garbage, most of which ends up in landfills. We heat our homes in the winter and run the air conditioning when the summer heat becomes intolerable. Out of necessity, many of us drive and, worse still, fly! When taking an Eco Quiz to test my carbon footprint, I discovered that if everyone on the planet lived the way I do, we would need **six planets** to provide the necessary resources. This was a shock to me since I make every effort to live sustainably; however, I also travel by plane and this negatively affected my Eco Quiz scores. Am I going to stop traveling? No. Am I therefore culpable regarding the proliferation of greenhouse gasses? Yes, and undeniably so.

 What is significant is not so much the originality of *Laudato Si'* as Pope Francis' insistence that the reasons our planet has become an "immense pile of filth" (#21) are insatiable consumerism, rampant individualism, a throw away culture, exploitation of the poor, a utilitarian view of Nature and the failure to see the interconnectedness of all life forms. Those who consume, slash and burn have no sense of the sacred. They may be religiously observant, but there is a complete disconnect on their part when it comes to their unsustainable behaviors and morality. And, at some level, this is true for most of us: we enjoy convenience and creature comforts and seldom connect the price others (human or otherwise) are paying to keep us happy! When I purchase new clothing online, for example, I am blissfully unaware as to whether the garment in question was made in a sweat shop; my priorities, in fact, are color, style, expected fit and price! These driving consumer concerns are precisely what perpetuate the sweat shop phenomenon— the only way manufacturers can satisfy consumer demands is to work their laborers harder, in grim conditions, while paying them less!

out of control > ?
not need but demand

The encyclical points out that those with the ability to make a difference often lack "political will" because they do not wish to lose the support of Big Business. The unholy alliance between politics and economics means that public figures may resort to "green rhetoric," but their approach to solving problems is "band-aid" at best, often masking the scope of environmental damage for which certain mega-corporations are responsible (#49). If a politician has received a hefty contribution to the campaign chest, then he or she is more likely to turn a blind eye when the donor's wealth is derived from socially unjust practices. We saw this when the first medical reports came out about the dangers of consuming tobacco. By 1986, the US Navy took a stand against the use of tobacco and set a goal of being "tobacco free" by the year 2000. This is what happened when lobbyists and Congress combined to torpedo this initiative:

> However, efforts to restrict tobacco sales and use aboard the USS Roosevelt prompted tobacco industry lobbyists to persuade their allies in Congress to legislate that all naval ships must sell tobacco. Congress

~ 22 ~

also removed control of ships' stores from the Navy. By 1993, the Navy abandoned its smoke-free goal entirely and promised smokers a place to smoke on all ships. Congressional complicity in promoting the agenda of the tobacco industry thwarted the Navy's efforts to achieve a healthy military workforce.
(http://www.ncbi.nlm.nih.gov/pubmed/2123 3435)

Sadly, in every age, politicians from all over the world have been willing to sell their birth right, the rights of others and the rights of future generations in the interests of accruing personal wealth and power. And, perhaps even more sadly, we seldom find out the "real" story until the damage is done, for the simple reason that the same corrupt corporations who "own" the politicians also own the media and therefore control the news. Today, smokers know the risks that they take in lighting up, but how many thousands of people have died because 1) they were assured that smoking was safe and 2) tobacco companies deliberately targeted youth, not only making cigarettes seem "cool," but also lacing them with addictive substances?

Pope Francis has an agenda for "every person living on this planet" (#3). What he calls for is nothing less than "ecological conversion." He makes a passionate plea for sustainable living, for an end to sins against creation, for new policies that will serve humanity rather than destroy it. Just as *The Global Ethic* of The Parliament of the World's Religions (1993) called for a complete transformation of consciousness in response to the world's agony, so Pope Francis is appealing for a "new and universal solidarity" (#14). He writes as a spiritual leader whose task is to awaken consciences and save humanity from self-destruction. In other words, he is doing exactly what his detractors want him to do—saving souls!

But my task is not to provide a synopsis of what may become the defining encyclical of Francis' papacy; nor is this book a *"Cliff's Notes"* to the document. At the same time, I am not undertaking a merely promotional role here, though some may see it as such. On the contrary, I hope most of my readers are already familiar with the encyclical— reading it for oneself is really the only way to do it justice, and, contrary to Chris Jackson's assessment, it *is* a document well worth the time.

Even if you have only read brief excerpts or have merely read about **Laudato Si'** in the media, you may have been moved enough to want to use it in your preaching or teaching. *preach* To do so, however, is not a matter of political correctness, but one of passionate commitment, the willingness to *live* the message and not just talk about it. I am writing for those, from any faith, who want to take the next step, in other words, for those who feel called, as I do, to advance Pope Francis' plea for ecological conversion, a new heart.

In the following chapters, I offer suggestions for incorporating *Laudato Si'* in church and classroom. As a seasoned preacher/teacher myself, I understand the vast influence each of us can have through our words. There is a Zen saying that when a butterfly flaps a wing, some positive impact happens as a consequence on the other side of the globe. Here I am flapping both wings, hoping you will do the same!

Many Blessings,

Elizabeth

Elizabeth-Anne Stewart
Chicago, June 19th, 2015

REALITY

"Reality," Eliot would say,
"is too much for humankind."
Now, I know what he meant:
when all things are in focus,
sharply delineated,
freed from shadows,
when one's ears are unstopped
and one's cataracts removed,
then the knife
twists in the soul
bringing deeper clarity still
like too much sun
on a ski slope
or intense light
after anesthesia.
Dark glasses lost,
I perceive how others
avoid my burning gaze
as though afraid
of what I may reveal,
afraid, too, of the contagion

that rawness brings
when there is too much
to bear…

Elizabeth-Anne Stewart. *Woman Dreamer*,

CHAPTER ONE

Living the Message, Becoming the Messenger

Perhaps you have turned to this book to save yourself the trouble of having to read *Laudato Si'*. Perhaps you feel compelled to climb on the encyclical bandwagon because it is the politically correct thing to do, or because "higher ups" have demanded compliance. Or perhaps you so love the Earth that you welcome the opportunity to share that love with others. While I do not wish to discourage anyone from exploring how to preach and teach *Laudato Si'*, the only way to be authentic in either role is to *live* the message.

Self-education is crucial here. For some readers, *Laudato Si'* provides a synthesis of material with which they are already familiar. The examples provided, the terminology used and even the scriptural framework may offer revision rather than revelation. The text becomes an opportunity to pause and reflect on what they already know; moreover, such readers bring to the text their own body of knowledge and this, in turn, amplifies the text. For example, when Section II refers to the loss of bio-diversity, an informed reader may be aware of the importance of crop genetic diversity in averting world famine. As James K. Boyce, author of *Economics, the Environment and Our Common Wealth*, points out, "diversity is what enables plant breeders today to respond to outbreaks of new insect pests and crop diseases by finding resistant varieties"(5).

Or when the encyclical refers to the threat to marine life (#40), informed readers may be aware of the massive accumulation of micro-plastics in our oceans, the best known of which is commonly called the Pacific Garbage Patch. These gyres of marine debris are responsible for the deaths of countless sea birds, turtles and fish; the same micro-plastics that kill jelly fish and baby albatross make their way into our food chain, so that we, too, are ingesting toxic chemicals.

If you belong to this category of readers, then *Laudato Si'* offers affirmation and support. Finally, the church (or rather, its leader!) has taken a firm stand on issues that have concerned you for years, if not decades. Now, you can enjoy knowing that you are not alone in caring for "our common home." In fact, you might feel inspired to become more involved in promoting a "green" agenda, perhaps even through your faith community. If before you felt on the fringes, now you are "main stream," no longer "eccentric" but "ahead of your times"!

In contrast, other readers may find themselves in completely unfamiliar territory; they bring nothing to the text because they have had little exposure to a "green agenda." Terms such as "sustainable living," "renewable energy," "ecological debt," and "environmental footprint" might as well be a foreign language. To comprehend the encyclical, these readers have to de-code "the jargon," simply to untangle the points being presented. For

them, the task of reading *Laudato Si'*
understandably becomes more formidable
and time consuming, creating frustration,
anger and even a sense of inadequacy.

But all is not lost! If you, yourself, feel "left
behind" in terms of the concepts presented
or if you are unsure as to where you stand on
some of the issues, take the text slowly and
absorb it in small chunks. No one is going to
examine you on your knowledge base or
expect you to have a built in "green
vocabulary." As you read, you may want to
make a list of unfamiliar terms, together
with some of the more striking allusions, as
for example, the effects of the oil industry
on the Niger Delta. Where, first of all, is the
Niger Delta? Who lives there? What has
been the people's experience since Shell and
other petroleum companies began polluting
the wetlands?

The amazing reality is that once we develop
an interest in one ecological issue, we
suddenly discover new ones, almost by
osmosis. At least, that is how it has been for

me. Years ago, as an undergraduate student at the University of Malta, I volunteered at an international ecology conference that focused on pollution in the Mediterranean; that was my first exposure to the possible "death" of a sea. I don't recall my exact responsibilities at that conference, but I do remember the shock I felt as I listened to speaker after speaker present evidence that my beloved Mediterranean could soon become too toxic to sustain life! Because my eyes had opened to the consequences of toxic waste, I suddenly began to see countless other problems that I had previously either ignored or dismissed as unimportant.

Of course, each preacher or teacher's comfort level with the document is going to be different, but without a basic understanding of the concepts presented, it will be impossible to be the messenger. Not only do I recommend a thorough reading of *Laudato Si'*, but also supplemental reading such as *Blessed Unrest* to which I referred in the introduction. Hawken's book is not only informative, but it also has a remarkable appendix of over 100 pages which defines key terms in the ecological movement. Highly readable, the book presents good news as well as bad, helping the reader move beyond despair to finding attainable solutions.

Becoming informed, then, is the first step in preaching or teaching this encyclical. No less important, however, is our commitment to ecological conversion on a personal level. Some readers may already be living sustainably, though there is always room for improvement; most, I suspect, will have given little thought to their ecological footprint. While today's youth are familiar with the 3R's—**REDUCE, RE-CYCLE, RE-USE**— previous generations tend to be oblivious. Here, in America, the 3 R's seem diametrically opposed to the American Dream. Many, having been raised with a sense of entitlement, assume that if they can pay for something, they can use it and dispose of it as they please. A two year old iPhone? Time for the landfill! A scratch on the SUV's bumper? Time for a trade-in! A 65," full HD, LED, 3D flat screen TV? Time to shelve out $4,999.00 and purchase a75" model!

While many of us are accustomed to "inner work," and regularly spend time in self-reflection, it has not been our tradition to include "sins against creation" in our examination of conscience. For other faith traditions, care of the created world and ethics go hand in hand. The ancient Egyptians, for example, believed they would be judged in the afterlife on sins against creation; the forty-two *Negative Confessions* include the following declarations of innocence:

> I have not caught fish with bait made of the bodies of the same kind of fish.
> I have not stopped water when it should flow.
> I have not made a cutting in a canal of running water.

I have not waded in water (i.e. polluted the Nile).

The Egyptian Book of the Dead
(http://reshafim.org.il/ad/egypt/negative_confessions/index.html)

Similarly, Judaism insists that those who are living should leave the world in such a way that it can be enjoyed by the next seven generations. Another beautiful *mitzvot* or commandment is the obligation for each believer to be engaged in *"Tikkun Olam"*—that is, in the repair of the world. Rabbi Isaac Luria, a Jewish mystic, taught that:

> …it is the task of each person to redeem and liberate the sacred that lies within every material form, animate and inanimate. From stones and plants to animals, ourselves and one another— a heavenly Exile exists until the Light returns unbroken to its Source. (Hoffman 97)

Perhaps the most developed understanding of the sacredness of creation is to be found in the beliefs and traditions of primal peoples. Chief Seattle, in response to the United States Government's inquiry about buying tribal lands (c. 1855), is reputed to have written a marvelous letter which epitomizes the world view of the Salish tribes from around the Puget Sound. Though there is controversy regarding the authorship of this letter, it nevertheless provides insight into an Earth-based spirituality very different from that of traditional Christianity:

> This we know: the Earth does not belong to man; man belongs to the Earth. All things are connected like the blood that unites us all. Man did not weave the web of life; he is merely a strand in it. Whatever he does to the web, he does to himself. One thing we know: our God is also your God. The Earth is precious to him and to harm the Earth is to heap contempt on its Creator. (Campbell 34)

What we see in this excerpt is tribal consciousness rather than the rugged individualism of the modern era. Here, the community is primary, but community does not simply refer to humanity but to all creation. The image of the spider's web— traditionally a feminine image— reflects both interconnectedness and inter-dependence. In this scheme of things, humanity is *part* of creation rather than the center of creation. The Great Spirit weaves the web, delighting in this handiwork, and any break, however infinitesimal, wounds the Divine Heart.

Sadly, Christianity, though originating in a Jewish matrix, has no such rich tradition of caring for the Earth, mostly because of the influence of Hellenism on the early church. Although the Hebrew scriptures assert the goodness of creation, as for example in Genesis and the Psalms, and although Jesus himself was an "outdoors man" who drew much of his imagery from Nature, by the second century, only the spiritual realm seemed to hold value. The Platonic idea that the soul is imprisoned in the body resulted in a negative attitude towards the physical universe (*Phaedo, 82d-e*), while Aristotle's writing set the stage for negativity towards women; in *Politics I:V*, he declares, "as regards the sexes, the male is by Nature superior and the female inferior, the male ruler and the female subject." In *The Generation of Animals*, he supports this position by explaining that women are nothing more than "impotent males" because they cannot produce semen (XX).

Negative views towards the body, towards women, towards Nature filtered into Christian theology and Christian spirituality. The "world" was evil; the flesh required mortification; Nature was there to serve a utilitarian purpose rather than to be enjoyed; women were "unclean," and, according to Tertullian, were "the devil's gateway." The purpose of life was to suffer in a vale of tears, so that after being tried and tested, worthy believers could ascend to their heavenly reward. Even the great medieval saint, Francis of Assisi, who is renowned for his love of animals and Nature in general, punished his flesh so severely that before he died, he begged pardon of "Brother Ass" (his name for his body).

To this day, many Christians —and in particular, pre-Vatican II Catholics— are the product of such world-negating views. Until the 1960's, religious formation for clergy and religious communities was typically based on long hours of prayer, hard work, self-denial and penance. In the lay experience, spirituality entailed stoic acceptance of suffering, fulfilling religious obligations and avoiding the fires of hell. Missing mass on Sunday or forgetting to fast on Good Friday would unquestionably have been "mortal sins," but taking a forty-five minute hot shower would merely have been considered self-indulgent.

Laudato Si' turns upside down not only our attitudes towards Nature, but also our understanding of our place in the cosmos and of what it means to be human; it also invites us to embrace a spirituality that recognizes the Reign of God right here on Earth and not just in the afterlife. It is a revolutionary text which calls into question all our previous assumptions about the universe: we are no longer free to exploit the Earth and her resources, both animate and inanimate, but are called to careful stewardship of all life. The Earth, in fact, is a sacrament of God's presence, a reality that both St. Francis and St. Bonaventure were aware of more than 800 years ago. In *The Soul's Journey into God,* Bonaventure writes: "In relation to our position in creation, the universe itself is a ladder by which we can ascend into God" (60). To behold the beauty of creation, then, is the first step towards beholding the Beauty of God!

It always is difficult to embrace a new mindset, to undergo a transformation of consciousness, but especially when one has held certain beliefs for decades. Logically speaking, older preachers are therefore likely to have greater difficulty accepting **Laudato Si'** than their younger counterparts.

Likewise, senior faculty in universities and seminaries may also face more challenges than young teachers in an elementary school setting. Of course, there are always exceptions. Sometimes, the elderly among us are the most informed and the most open minded!

Regardless of age, ecological conversion involves assessing our lifestyles in terms of sustainability. To preach and teach *Laudato Si'* authentically, we need to believe our own message and to live by the same ethical principles we expect of others. By modeling behaviors and attitudes that reflect a loving concern for the environment, we leave a greater impact on the world than anything mere words can accomplish.

CHAPTER TWO

Mea Culpa! Assessing Our Ecological Footprint

In Catholic tradition, the first stage in seeking forgiveness is repentance, but we cannot repent if we are unaware of what we have done (or failed to do); nor can we avoid sins against creation in the future, if we continue to be oblivious. To help clarify what is sinful about our behaviors, Pope Francis cites Ecumenical Patriarch Bartholomew:

> "For human beings… to destroy the biological diversity of God's creation; for human beings to degrade the integrity of the Earth by causing changes in its climate, by stripping the Earth of its natural forests or destroying its wetlands; for human beings to contaminate the Earth's waters, its land, its air, and its life— these are sins." (#8)

"Well," we might say to ourselves, smugly, *"There's no way **I'm** to blame for Global Warming and the rest of the world's ills. Why! I even recycle newspaper and have stopped using plastic bags!"* As long as this is our conviction, we will be poor ambassadors for **Laudato Si'**. We may point the finger at BP for its contamination of the Gulf and at Shell Oil for destroying much of the Niger Delta, but then we turn a blind eye to our own squandering of energy. We may decry unfair labor practices in Third World factories, but we continue to purchase cheap clothing and electronics that have been made in the equivalent of slave labor camps. We express shock at the cruel treatment of animals in factory farms, but pile on the bacon and demand the beef! We lament the disappearance of bees and butterflies, but insist on spraying garden pests with a cocktail of Roundup and other chemicals....

Taking a cue from the ancient Egyptians, I have put together a series of 42 *positive* and 42 *negative* statements to help us in our examination of conscience. Just as the heart of the deceased would be weighed at the final judgment to see if that person had lived according to the principles of *Ma'at* or justice, so we, too, might imagine our hearts being weighed by God the Creator. The stakes are high. For the ancient Egyptian, if the heart were heavier than the Feather of Justice which lay on the great golden scales of Osiris, it would be devoured by the monstrous Ammit (part god, part croc, part rhino, part leopard); there would be no after life, no Field of Reeds, but only non-existence. For us, if we are found wanting, the judgment will not only be in the world to come, but in the here and now, for unless we change our ways, the Earth will no longer be able to sustain life as we know it.

I invite you now to read through this **Positive and Negative Confession,** so as to see how many points you agree with (the more the better). Depending upon whether you live in community or are single, whether you are married with children or a grandparent, whether you live in your own home or under someone else's roof, you may find that many of the statements do not fit your life experience. At the same time, the list is not comprehensive— there must be countless points that, I, in my own oblivion, have overlooked. You will note that some of the questions have to do with how we treat other humans; this is because we are *part* of Nature, not separate from it, or "over" it. I should add the **Confession** was spontaneously generated and that therefore the questions are not in any particular order, hierarchical or otherwise.

I encourage you to take a holistic look at *your* responses; in this way you can assess whether you are a good steward of creation or an ecological sinner! There are no points to tally, no categories to indicate whether you belong to the *"good, the bad or the ugly"*— you, yourself, will know what needs to be done or left undone! The point is not to make anyone feel guilty, inadequate or embarrassed; rather, the goal is to help preachers and teachers reflect on their own relationship with the Earth and to make the changes that will improve that relationship.

Imagine yourself now, standing at the pearly gates, waiting for St. Peter to let you in. He holds the sacred Keys in one hand and a lie-detector machine in the other. Behind him are three pearly white steps leading to *Thy Kingdom Come*; behind you, to the left, is a flight of black stairs leading into the place of eternal wailing and gnashing of teeth while, to the right, another flight of red stairs leads to a high powered sauna where sinners sweat out the last vestiges of imperfection. You await your turn, knowing that any attempt at deception will result in changes to your blood pressure, pulse and respiration. *And now it's time!*

The Positive Confession

1. I check the labels of the products I buy to make sure they were produced under Fair Trade conditions.

2. I walk, bike or share transportation rather than drive alone.

3. I plan my errands so as to drive as little as possible.

4. I take my own re-usable shopping bags to the store.

5. I recycle all consumable goods that are recyclable e.g. paper, plastic, glass etc.

6. I dispose of small electronics and batteries at locations which handle these items.

7. I re-use packaging, gift wrap and other such items rather than buying new.

8. I repair things I own such as worn shoes and damaged luggage rather than replacing them.

9. I participate in boycotts against companies that engage in inhumane labor practices or in policies that damage the environment.

10. I use environmentally safe household products.

11. I use environmentally safe personal products.

12. I open my windows rather than use air conditioning.

13. I keep the temperature of my home below 68oF in the winter.

14. I drive a fuel-efficient car.

15. I purchase large appliances that are eco-friendly.

16. I pay my bills online to avoid paper consumption.

17. I buy only what I need and avoid waste and duplication.

18. I give away what I am no longer using.

19. I only replace products when they no longer function, not when there's something better on the market.

20. I hang my laundry out to dry rather than use a dryer.

21. I decorate my home with eco-friendly paint and flooring.

22. I use Eco-smart bulbs to save electricity.

23. I use recycled paper products.

24. I purchase Fair Trade gift items to benefit Third World artisans.

25. I limit my use of paper towels and use cleaning cloths instead.

26. I unplug my TV, computer and small appliances when I am not using them to avoid "vampire electricity."

27. I buy organic food.

28. I'm vegetarian or vegan, or have reduced my meat consumption.

29. I buy food that is locally grown.

30. I take my clothes to a "Green Cleaner" rather than a regular dry cleaner.

31. I re-use scrap paper.

32. I take short showers.

33. I save rain water and water from washing fruit and veggies to water my plants.

34. I re-use my bath towels several times before washing them.

35. I find natural solutions for pest control.

36. I use leftovers to create compost for my garden.

37. I make sure the faucets aren't leaking and that the toilet tank isn't running.

38. I control the temperature in my home with blinds, curtains or shutters.

39. I adopt pets from shelters rather than deal with breeders or puppy mills.

40. I grow some of my own food.

41. I only use green vendors for my home and garden.

42. I always look for the "natural solution."

The Negative Confession

1. I do not travel by air unnecessarily so as to limit my carbon footprint.

2. I do not waste food.

3. I do not use leaf blowers and other polluting equipment.

4. I do not purchase bottled water but filter tap water instead.

5. I do not use disposable plates, cups, napkins etc.

6. I do not print more than is necessary.

7. I do not turn on lights unless I am in the room.

8. I do not vote for politicians who favor Big Business over the environment.

9. I do not harm living creatures unless they threaten my safety and wellbeing.

10. I do not invest in companies that manufacture weapons or promote unjust labor practices.

11. I do not waste water.

12. I do not pollute water.

13. I do not cause others to weep.

14. I do not create litter.

15. I do not remain silent when others are creating litter.

16. I do not remain silent when others are abusing animals.

17. I do not remain silent when others are discriminated against.

18. I do not participate in stereotyping and ethnic jokes.

19. I do not purchase brands responsible for human suffering or the suffering of animals.

20. I do not purchase brands responsible for environmental damage.

21. I do not use plastic grocery bags.

22. I do not purchase GMO foods.

23. I do not buy consumer goods unnecessarily.

24. I do not throw out what others can use.

25. I do not smoke.

26. I do not cause air pollution by burning leaves, having a faulty exhaust system etc.

27. I do not use chemicals if there is an alternative.

28. I do not use over the counter drugs if there is a home remedy.

29. I do not "keep up with the Jones's."

30. I do not purchase cut Christmas Trees.

31. I do not create noise pollution.

32. I do not release balloons at outdoor events.

33. I do not dump my garbage in recycling bins.

34. I do not cook/eat foods which entail the suffering of animals (e.g. lobster, veal, *foie gras* etc.)

35. I do not euthanize old pets for my convenience.

36. I do not buy furniture with leather upholstery.

37. I do not buy products that involve child labor.

38. I do not consume chocolate and coffee if they are not Fair Trade.

39. I do not remain ignorant about world events.

40. I do not turn my back on the hungry and homeless.

41. I do not treat others as if their lives are less important than my own.

42. I don't act as though I own the universe.

Now pause for reflection. Will St. Peter let you in to *Thy Kingdom Come,* or are you doomed to one place of suffering or the other? What do **YOU** think you deserve? Would you say you respect the environment, take it for granted or abuse it— or a little of each? Have the *Positive and Negative Confessions* helped you reflect on your own stewardship of creation? If so, what have you learned? Do you feel affirmed or have you been found wanting?

What changes, however small, are *you* willing to implement for the sake of the planet we call our home? I encourage you to record some practical goals that you can put into immediate practice— even *one* goal would be a step in the right direction. Feel free to share this examination of conscience with others; if you are a teacher, this is something you could use in the classroom to generate conversation. Students of all ages love taking non-graded quizzes that reveal something about themselves— this quiz might be a first step in promoting ecological values in a non-threatening way!

A Prayer for Ecological Sinners

Loving God,

All creation is filled with your glory, from the smallest beetle to the mightiest elephant, from the humblest of flowers to the loftiest mountain. Each creature has a place in the circle of life; each plant provides beauty and sustains this circle with essential nutrients. Nothing you have created is insignificant; nothing is without value. Every stone, every blade of grass, reflects your love for the Earth; every fish, every bird and every mammal reminds us of your creativity.

We thank you for the wonders of this world, for the amazing planet you have entrusted to us. Open our eyes to your Presence in Nature as well as in ourselves. Help us to see the uniqueness of each living being and to appreciate the variety that dazzles each landscape.

Humbly, we ask your forgiveness for those times when we have cared more for ourselves than for future generations. We recognize how greed has turned us into heartless consumers who feed on the misery of the poor. We apologize for treating the Earth as a thing to be exploited and for using and abusing your children in the name of progress. We repent for having felled the forests and leveled the mountains, for destroying habitats and causing species to become extinct, for polluting the oceans and poisoning the land, for making the air toxic with smog and acid rain. We are sorry for our carelessness, for having taken our planet for granted, for our lack of gratitude.

You have been infinitely generous to us, O God. Give us new hearts—hearts big enough to hold the world and all its creatures. Teach us how to repair the damage we have done that the Earth may become your sanctuary once more, a garden of delight for all creatures, great and small.

We pray in Jesus' Name,

AMEN

CHAPTER THREE

Preaching to the Choir

To preach to the choir implies that the very people in front of you have already got the message. Those in the assembly do not require education or convincing. On the contrary, they share your perspective and may be considerably more knowledgeable than you are. In some ways, having an ecologically informed audience makes your task easier. First of all, you don't have to worry about being heckled or accused of meddling in politics; it is also unlikely that anyone will walk out in the middle of your homily, creating a raucous in the process. The good news is that you have a friendly, sympathetic audience. Secondly, there is no need to spend hours in research so as to present "the facts" and educate the ignorant. They already know what you know— maybe more! All this means they will be willing to listen to you.

So you stride out confidently and at ease, microphone in hand— but **what** do you say? We have already ruled out that your task is neither to educate nor to persuade. And you certainly do not want to bore everyone by regurgitating the same old examples and doomsday warnings they have heard 1,000 times. This audience already knows that if the polar ice caps melt, there will be catastrophic coastal flooding and that Manhattan, Florida, and other low-lying areas will be under water. It knows that if the population of honey bees continues to be decimated, there will be global famine— Einstein, in fact, once predicted that the death of the honey bee would lead to the annihilation of humanity within a four year period! And it knows, too well, that Americans make up only 5% of the world's population but produce 50% of the globe's solid waste! There is no point, therefore, in spewing out statistics— your audience will quickly become disengaged.

The starting point for any preacher who wishes to preach on *Laudato Si'* to an

ecologically-aware audience is to have a
clear agenda. If you are not going to
proselytize, what *are* you going to do? I
suggest a couple of approaches:

1) **To affirm the assembly for caring
   about the Earth and for grieving
   over ecological destruction.** Those
   who weep and mourn need to know
   that their tears *are* prayer and that
   God hears the cries of the poor. The
   ability to grieve over suffering
   creation aligns our hearts with God's
   heart, so that our suffering and God's
   suffering become one and the same
   suffering, just as our outrage and
   God's outrage are one and the same
   outrage. This sounds very simple,
   perhaps even unimportant. However,
   I believe that those who grieve over
   the agony of the world need to
   experience solidarity with others,
   especially within their faith
   community. Their grief, in fact, is an
   expression of their faith and can

draw them closer to God. They will appreciate being reminded of this.

2) **To acknowledge how overwhelming the issues are, while encouraging the assembly to find some way of making an impact, no matter how small**. *The Beatitudes* teach us that weeping and mourning are signs of being blessed, but blessing is also to be found in working for social justice. There will be people in the "choir assembly" who feel completely helpless in the face of the world's agony. Whether because of age, illness, financial difficulties or obligations towards dependents, some parishioners may feel they have nothing to contribute. As preacher, you can assure everyone that one person *can* make a difference. You might even make suggestions as to concrete steps individuals can take, or what the parish might do as a community of caring believers. Such suggestions

would be very welcome to those who want to "do something" but have no idea how to go about it. Rather than providing facts, as preacher you may find yourself becoming more of a facilitator or guide.

3) **To help the assembly move from despair to spiritual empowerment**. True empowerment comes not from *our* efforts but from allowing the Spirit of God to move freely in us, through us and with us. Creation is groaning in one great act of giving birth (Rom 8: 23) and the Spirit is surely the midwife of this birthing! We need to believe that with God all things are possible, and that our tears and prayers will hasten the birth of a New Earth. As preacher, you can frame the present suffering of the planet in terms of Paschal Mystery: a terrible dying is taking place but, through God's grace, there will be resurrection! This is an opportunity for faith-sharing and faith-building,

for moving parishioners from being merely religiously observant to having a dynamic Christian spirituality that meets the demands of the C21st.

Each of these approaches allows you, the preacher, to express your feelings and concerns and to stand *with* the people rather than as a detached bystander or "know-it-all." Moreover, each approach can be used with children and adults alike during Sunday liturgies in Ordinary Time as well as during the liturgical seasons of Advent, Christmas, Lent and Easter. Holy Days such as Pentecost and Corpus Christi also offer wonderful opportunities for focusing on **Laudato Si',** as do communal penance services, devotions such as *The Stations of the Cross* and special occasions such as Earth Day, the Feast of St. Francis of Assisi and Mother's Day ("Mother Earth").

Preaching, of course, begins with the scripture readings of the day as well as with "The Liturgy of Life" – in other words, with major events on the world's stage or in the local community. Even if a Sunday is designated as *"Laudato Si' Sunday,"* the preacher should not overlook these two requirements. At the same time, preaching needs to be "organic," and any attempt to twist a text to fit a message simply doesn't work. The preaching, in fact, will sound contrived and any scriptural references will seem "tacked on." When possible, it is therefore advisable to select a Sunday when the readings themselves fit in well with themes of sustainable living and ecological conversion.

Looking through the lectionary for YEAR B, for example, I found myself drawn to the readings for **October 11th, 2015.** The first reading is Wisdom 7:7-11, a passage extolling the beauty of Wisdom:

> "Yet all good things come to me in her company,
> countless riches at her hands."

The Responsorial Psalm, Ps. 90, is a psalm of praise that includes the lines:

"How long, O Lord, before you return?
Pity your servants,
Shine your love on us each dawn,
And gladden all our days." (13-14)

The Second Reading, Hebrews 4:12-13, speaks of God's ability to know our secret thoughts and raises the issue of accountability:

"No creature can hide from God but everything is naked and exposed to the eyes of the One to whom we must render an account."

And finally, the Gospel itself is that well-known story from Mark's gospel in which a rich man asks,

"Good teacher, what must I do to inherit eternal life?" (Mk 10:17-30)

Immediately, my preacher's "light bulb" goes on! In fact, the readings themselves

provide the outline of the homily; it could go
something like this:

1. Lacking Wisdom we have chosen
    profit over truth, greed over
    compassion, power over prudence
    and pride over humility. We have
    made gods of ourselves to the
    detriment of our planet.

2. We cannot hide from God or deny
    our culpability. Each of us, to a
    greater or lesser extent, is to blame
    for the scourges afflicting Earth;
    each of us is accountable.

3. We cry out to God to intervene, but
    we are the ones who must undergo a
    change of heart.

4. Some, like the rich man in the
    gospel, will find this too challenging
    and simply return to their old ways.
    Others, will take an honest self-
    inventory that includes sins against
    the environment. As a result, they
    may be willing to divest themselves

of all behaviors and possessions which are harmful to creation. The choice is ours: to go away sad like the rich man, or to build the Kingdom of God right here, in our midst.

Of course, all this needs to be fleshed out with details and examples. References to "The Liturgy of Life" could include speaking about a community issue such as the proposal for a new factory that will cause air pollution. Or if there has been a recent maritime oil spill or a freight train derailment involving a cargo of chemicals, then these events can also be woven into the fabric of the homily. You are the weaver and the color and texture of your tapestry will be absolutely unique!

Laudato Si' is such a rich document that a single Sunday approach will not do it justice. One suggestion would be for the preaching team to identify the key themes it wishes to emphasize over the course of the liturgical year. These themes should be presented from a spiritual perspective rather than from the viewpoint of social activism or politics; also, they may be secondary rather than primary themes, sometimes nothing more than a brief "aside." During Lent, for example, the topic of sins against the environment may be one focus. A homily based on the story of *The Samaritan Woman* (Jn 4:1-30) may invite the community to reflect on what it means to thirst for the presence of God; at the same time, it may remind those present that many of the world's people thirst for access to clean water. There is not only a spiritual message here – Jesus is the Living Water that satisfies all thirsts—but the homily also challenges the assembly to be more aware in terms of excessive water consumption.

Or take the story of *The Man Born Blind* (Jn 9:1-41), a healing narrative which is more about spiritual blindness than physical limitation. We cannot hope to advance spiritually when we cling to distorted ways of seeing such as imagining we are the center of the universe or that other lives are of lesser value than our own! A skilled preacher will not only cover the usual spiritual implications of this story, but might invite us to open our eyes to the ways in which our demand for certain goods leads to child labor, human trafficking and even slavery! Again, the spiritual message should not be sacrificed here, but the gospel provides a wonderful opportunity to blend environmental awareness and social justice with God's living Word.

The possibilities for integrating **Laudato Si'** with individual scriptural texts, the liturgical seasons and "The Liturgy of Life" are endless. Communities that hold a *Good Friday Walk for Justice* could include staging one of *The Stations of the Cross* outside the corporate headquarters of some company notorious for its abuse of the environment. Parishes that traditionally celebrate the Easter Vigil might want to adapt the first reading —the Creation story (Gn1:1-22)— to communicate the goodness of creation. The refrain, *"And God saw how good it was,"* could be highlighted through music, through choral repetition, through community response, all the way through the text, with no further commentary required!

Women's History Month could be a time when preachers draw parallels between the abuse of the Earth and the global abuse of women; if a particular community has a high rate of domestic violence, this could also be a topic that can be addressed. *Black History Month,* on the other hand, might include commentary on the subtle forms that racism takes— the fact, for example, that minority neighborhoods have a disproportionately large number of toxic waste dumps in their backyard as well as more industrial pollution than predominately white communities. Again, the spiritual message must be primary. Jesus, for example, constantly reached out to oppressed women, raising them up from soul-destroying situations so they could lead full and active lives; similarly, he responded to the needs of Samaritans, Romans and Canaanites, demonstrating an all-inclusive love that would not tolerate discrimination.

On a final note, the preacher who is "preaching to the choir" might consider asking the choir to participate in the homily! If there are parishioners who have an area of expertise that might help bring home a point you wish to make, invite them to come forward! I don't suggest you do this spontaneously, but that you identify a few people whose voices need to be heard, that you let them know in advance what you are looking for and the amount of time you would like them to speak. You could, for example, invite several grandmothers and great-grand mothers to briefly share their concerns for future generations. You might invite a doctor or nurse to speak, very briefly, about the connection between air pollution and asthma, emphysema and lung cancer. You might invite members of the Sierra Club or Greenpeace to explain why caring for the Earth is, for them, a spiritual mandate. If there are young children present, you could ask them to share with the community one small thing each of them is doing to help heal Mother Earth. The testimony of babes, by the way, will have a greater impact than anything you could say!

CREATION

In that time, in that sacred time
before memory, before story
before God cradled the Earth
the Word was with God
speaking yet spoken
moving yet still
splitting light from darkness
coaxing life from void
dancing over the deep,
rippling waters with laughter.

And God said, "Let there be"
and there was
and there is
and there will be.
God's Word is deed.

In our time, in our sacred time
we remember God's Word
spoken tenderly—
born of flesh, born of spirit
bearing God, blazing Light.

And creation trembles at the mystery
at the power and the glory
for grace and truth are ours, Alleluia!

Elizabeth-Anne Stewart. *Woman Dreamer*

CHAPTER FOUR

Preaching to the Pews

When you address a gathering of hostile, close-minded people, then you might as well be preaching to the pews – there is no "choir" in sight! Just as ***Laudato Si'*** was summarily dismissed by a few Catholic politicians who were quick to say that Pope Francis should leave science to scientists, so there will be communities that echo these sentiments— particularly if they are supporters of the said politicians! Without having read the encyclical, they will assume it is nothing more than a far left treatise on climate change, funded by misguided Democrats!

If the preacher ministering to such a community holds views that are diametrically opposed to those of the assembly, then there is the danger that 1) the preacher will feel alienated from the people; 2) the preacher will become judgmental towards the people; 3) the people will reject both the preacher and the preacher's message; 4) some of the people will stand with the preacher and some will stand against both preacher and their fellow parishioners. None of these, of course, are good scenarios. For preaching to divide a community defeats the purpose of Sunday liturgy. Now, that is not to say that you should avoid **awakening or challenging** the community, but divisions are seldom healthy and can lead to an "us v. them" atmosphere.

One would hope that balanced reporting by such publications as *Catholic World* will help the alienated move beyond their misgivings; William Patenaude, a columnist for the *Rhode Island Catholic* who writes at *Catholic Ecology.net*, has this to say:

> The focus of *Laudato Si'* is the human person. The central thesis is that the fallen Nature of the human heart and the resulting brokenness of human relations is the cause of the crises in our lives, families, nations, and now the life-sustaining eco-

systems that form our common home.

(http://www.catholicworldreport.com/Item/39 60/laudato_si_focuses_on_the_heart_of_man and_the_disorders_of_our_age.aspx)

Anyone who reads Patenaude's article will find a useful summary of the encyclical which captures its theological and ecological underpinnings. However, the author concedes that "there are statements in the encyclical that will successively upset, delight, and challenge most everyone." Ironically, the online commentary following his article proves just that, with such responses as *"fake science and false predictions of catastrophe"* being typical.

My suggestion is that in communities that are likely to be unreceptive, specific references to **Laudato Si'** should initially be presented in the parish bulletin or newsletter rather than during the homily. Though there are occasions when divisive issues *do* need to be addressed boldly and directly from the pulpit— as for example, racial incidents or gang violence within the community— other issues can be presented in a way that is more pastorally sensitive. Forcing the encyclical on those who are already convinced that it is a "papal mistake" is bound to cause conflict. If the assembly has already decided to see red, why produce an even redder flag during Sunday worship? It would be far better to introduce the document in non-threatening ways in which participation is entirely voluntary such as through articles, information sessions and even a discussion group. Efforts to educate the community need to be both intentional and thorough, focusing on every stratum of parish life, from liturgical ministry to CCD classes— but they don't have to happen during Sunday Mass!

This does not mean to say that the encyclical should not enjoy some preachable moments. On the contrary, you can creatively introduce many of its themes— without ever mentioning *Laudato Si'*, Pope Francis, Al Gore, global warming or climate change! Themes such as responsible stewardship, experiencing the Presence of God in creation (a Franciscan theme), and sustainable living as a spiritual path can be effortlessly woven into the homily. There is no need to give dire warnings of an approaching apocalypse or to adopt a "fire and brimstone" tone; rather, a more subtle way is needed here. Take, for example, the Advent season. Often, the readings themselves warn of catastrophic events to come, as on the First Sunday of Advent, Cycle B:

Jesus said to his disciples:
"There will be signs in the sun, the moon, and the stars,
and on Earth nations will be in dismay, perplexed by the roaring of the sea and the waves.
People will die of fright
in anticipation of what is coming upon the world,
for the powers of the heavens will be shaken."

Lk 21:25-28, 34-36

As preacher, the first thing NOT to say would be, "See! Even Jesus has predicted a bad outcome unless we change our ways!"

That would be the "red flag" approach. It would be wiser to acknowledge that both Christian tradition and scripture suggest the world will one day come to an end, but that how this will happen is debatable. There are those who say it will occur as part of an inevitable natural process; those who claim our sinfulness will advance the end days; and those who blame climate change. The cause, however, is irrelevant.

Then you could transition into the importance of "Staying awake" (Lk 21:35) and being vigilant at all times. How do we do this? Jesus himself provides the answer: to avoid drunken carousing and spiritual drowsiness. Disciples who are spiritually alert not only treat their brothers and sisters with compassion but also extend the same care to all creation. Rather than live in fear, we need to "prepare the way of the Lord" by avoiding consumerism, considering giving "alternative" or "Fair Trade" Christmas gifts, and planning Christmas festivities that are sustainable. Such an approach should give the assembly food for thought without aligning the preacher with "loony liberals." The message is both simple and scripturally based; there are no glaring ideologies at play but only an invitation to return to gospel values.

You can also introduce themes central to *Laudato Si'* via parish activities. During Advent, parishioners could be invited to make an ornament for the church Christmas tree representing some aspect of creation for which they are grateful. Or there could be a contest for the best Nativity scene made from trash (corks, cotton wool, bits of wire etc.) or from Nature (bark, twigs, seeds etc.) If the parish holds a Christmas craft fair, there could be a table devoted to environmentally-friendly gifts; another possibility would be to host a Fair Trade organization like *Ten Thousand Villages* which has an impressive catalogue of gifts that are hand made by Third World artisans.

Consciousness can be raised in many ways, not just through homilies. Like the exiled Duke in the Forest of Arden (Shakespeare.

As You Like It, Act 11 sc. 1), even the most closed-minded of parishioners can find

> "Tongues in trees, books in the running brooks,
> Sermons in stones, and good in everything."

Years ago, in the 1980's, I had first-hand experience of this when I visited a gallery exhibiting graphic photographs of those who had been abducted, tortured and murdered by the Death Squads of El Salvador. That one exhibit led me to conduct my own research on American involvement in Central America and to 1) become involved in peace activities; and 2) to introduce my students to alternative news sources regarding American foreign policy in such countries as Nicaragua, El Salvador, Honduras and Guatemala.

I remember using Nicholas Patricca's visionary play, *The Fifth Sun*, as a text in my English and Religion classes at DePaul University. Combining elements from tomb rituals and medieval morality plays,

Patricca's work depicts the journey of Oscar Romero, Archbishop of San Salvador, from detached scholar to courageous martyr. The independently produced film, *Romero*, staring Raul Julia, made for wonderful supplemental material and by the time the courses were over, a good number of the students had joined me in protest marches in downtown Chicago! Such is the power of art....

Over the years, I have read many "sermons in stones"— the *Aids Memorial Quilt* that began touring across the country in the late 1980's brought home the tragedy of lives taken too soon; the *Eyes Wide Open* exhibit in Grant Park, Chicago (2007), that consisted of the boots of fallen American soldiers, along with the shoes of Iraqi civilians, demonstrated the human cost of war; the *Off the Beaten Path* exhibit at Chicago's Cultural Center (2011) that highlighted art works depicting global violence against women, emphasized the consequences of misogyny....

Your task as preacher becomes easier when there is organizational support. With careful thought, "tongues in trees, books in the running brooks" can become an integral part of parish life. This, of course, needs to be a collaborative effort involving the entire leadership. The introduction of re-cycling bins on church property might seem like a small step but the visual reminder is perhaps more important than the actual success of the recycling program. Moving away from the use of church envelopes may again seem minor, but it, too, would make a non-threatening statement about the need to save paper. If the church employs a landscaping service, it might consider cancelling any use of chemicals or going with a "green" company. If there is space for an organic community garden, volunteers could assume responsibility for its care. And when hosting meetings or social gatherings, the church could find alternatives to the use of plastic bottles and styrofoam....

Over time, as church members become more environmentally aware, you, the preacher, will be able to speak directly about *Laudato Si'* without having to anticipate major backlash. Until that happens, however, the better approach is to deliver the message "indirectly"!

CHAPTER FIVE

Teaching Millennials

Teaching and preaching are two distinct activities, even if the content happens to be the same and the deliverer of the message functions in both roles, as I often do. The task of the preacher is to provide insight into the scriptures of the day, and to provide a message that applies to those present. This message can inspire, uplift, encourage, challenge and motivate; at some level, it should "wake up" the assembly, whether to renew discipleship, deepen compassion or lead to more honest self-reflection. Preaching, then, is not so much about transmitting information as about stirring the soul.

The task of the preacher is prophetic— not in the sense of predicting the future but in revealing "what is" and, in so doing, drawing the faithful closer to God's heart. In preaching on *Laudato Si'*, the preacher needs to establish spiritual and ethical connections between scripture and the document. It is not enough to summarize the contents of the encyclical because that approach is definitely out of place during liturgy. Rather, the focus should be to preach the encyclical in light of the Gospel.

Teaching, on the other hand, does not require an ethical, spiritual or scriptural perspective, especially in a secular setting. Of course, if you, as teacher, are willing and able to provide such a perspective, then that would be a plus in the learning environment. What is basic, however, is the transmission of facts, accurately and without bias, so that students can form critical judgments for themselves. No matter how passionate we are about environmental issues, it is never appropriate to brainwash those in our care or to grade them on our opinions. Our unique role is to provide a starting point for each student's own explorations.

I find Millennials —sometimes known as GenY— the perfect audience to work with. There is some fluidity in terms of who fits this definition, but the most commonly agreed upon age range seems to be those born between the early 1980's and early 2000's—in other words, today's young adults, college students and teenagers. Those of my generation, the Baby Boomers, are largely responsible for the environmental mess the world is experiencing today. Our parents, having experienced austerity because of WWII, were determined to give us everything that they themselves never had or had too little of. And so they gave; and so we consumed. Then, fat with the good things in life, we raised our Gen X children to feel entitled to their share of good life pie. Millennials, on the other hand, have inherited the consequences and are well aware of this.

We Baby Boomers and older Gen Xers are quick to judge Millennials for their obsession with technology, their lack of traditional academic skills, and their dependency on texting for communication. They are typically plugged in, constantly texting or surfing the net; they are known to multi-task and perform everyday activities online, from banking to shopping, from dating to seeking technical assistance. In general, Millennials are not great readers— most of their reading is done online in "small chunks." Few read the newspapers or books of any kind. They are used to scanning the internet for snippets of information, but would never curl up with a book for enjoyment. Before heading to college, many have had little experience reading any "heavy" material and few have ever written anything resembling a term paper. A fact that I find fascinating is that most will readily admit that they were never taught to write or read cursive writing— a problem for teachers who, like me, tend to scribble comments in the margins of student papers! In fact, when I return student work, I always give the class a few minutes to decipher my comments and to ask me to interpret what I have written. By way of an aside, although my students *could* submit their work digitally, I make copious comments that would take forever were I glued to my computer screen. I am definitely old fashioned here, but I like to sit at a table to grade papers, pen in hand. Much more contemplative that way.....

If you have taught Millennials, you will know that they find concentrating a challenge. They require a constant flow of ideas, images and activities. They get bored easily, and so you may have already adjusted your teaching style to accommodate them. Activities and discussions that would have interested Gen X students —my children's generation— definitely do not work with Millennials. However, if you can arouse their interest and create interesting assignments, then they will be engaged, perhaps passionately so!

But just because Millennials may not fit a Baby Boomer's definition of a "great student" does not mean to say that they lack positive characteristics. For example, I find them very open to learning about the problems facing the Earth and willing to make lifestyle changes that can make a difference. Though they tend to have little background in religion and have often been raised without a faith, they have spiritual values and believe in love, marriage, family and personal responsibility; they seek happiness more than things, want to travel, and are determined to live life on their own terms.

So why, you might ask, inflict *Laudato Si'* on those who, if left to their own devices, could never wade through the document? Well, Millennials are the generation that needs to fix things; they are voters, spenders and decision makers who have inherited a damaged Earth and need some guidance as to how to heal it. Since few will venture into places of worship, the classroom is the best place to reach out to them. You may already have tried strategies of your own, but I would like to share some approaches that I have found useful in working with this demographic.

In a religious environment— a Catholic university, for example— it would be possible to assign the encyclical as a textbook. Of course, a Religious Studies course would lend itself well to this, especially a course in Catholic Studies; however, unless text books are "pre-set," an instructor could select the encyclical for many other Humanities courses, including English, Sociology, Women's Studies and Environmental Studies. The benefit of assigning this to a Religious Studies course is that you would be free to examine the religious framework of the document in the context of faith formation.

Regardless of the course involved, my approach would be to divide the class into groups and have each group responsible for a section of the document. Their task would be to identify key terms, key concepts, major problems being presented, the cause of these problems, possible solutions to these problems and, finally, their own "take" on what they have read, including opposing viewpoints. Each group would then present its findings to the entire class. Participants would be encouraged to use audio-visual resources to support their oral presentations;

they would also incorporate personal experience with the issue being discussed.

This format —one which I have used in many classes— means that everyone is actively involved in the learning process but that the task of intensive reading will be shared. Here, there is room for discussion, critical thinking, research and creative presentations. Students could be graded, as a group, on the presentations or could also hand in "group notes," or a "group essay," with accountability checks to ensure that everyone has contributed equally. As instructor, you might prefer to split the grade between group presentations/individual written assignments— there are many ways of providing fair assessment.

In a secular university or college, it would be difficult to justify using *Laudato Si'* as a text, unless the school had a Religious Studies Department. Then, of course, the focus would not be on the faith dimensions of the document but its social implications; whether religiously observant or not, you would be obliged to treat the encyclical as an "artifact," rather than as a theological statement. The separation of Church & State means that any professor would have to tread very carefully so as to maintain objectivity and not offend non-believing students!

Even if the encyclical itself never makes it into the classroom, there are countless ways in which we can incorporate its main themes in our teaching. For over a decade, I have consciously inserted environmental concerns into course syllabi, and am gratified that Millennials appreciate being exposed to the critical issues facing our world. My starting point is to introduce topics that directly affect them and their families. First on the list is FOOD. At Roosevelt University, Chicago, where I teach English, I have recently made FOOD the research topic for a course in College Writing. The syllabus reads:

Research Topics

All 8-10 page research papers will focus on some aspect of **Food** and will present a clearly defined position. Together we will generate a comprehensive list of possibilities, but here are some suggestions:

Food Deserts; GMO Crops; Factory Farming; The Use of Hormones and Pesticides in Animal Feed; Fluoride in Drinking Water; Fast Foods and Obesity; Anorexia; The Death of Bees and Global Famine; Raw Food Diets; Fad Diets; Becoming Vegan or Vegetarian; Fast Foods and Global Warming; Sugar and Slavery; the Thai Fishing Industry and Slavery; Child Labor and Chocolate; Cesar Chavez and the Grape Boycott; Cocoa Cola and Toxic Waste; Maintaining Health Through diet etc.

Class discussions build on what students already know. For example, minority students can speak firsthand about the consequences of living in a food desert, that is, in a location where there are no grocery stores because food chains such as Jewels or Whole Foods tend to shy away from high-crime areas or economically depressed locations. One student described how her grandmother never had healthy food on hand. Without a car and unable to bring home bags of groceries on public transportation, she stocked up her refrigerator at the local gas station. There, she could purchase potato chips, white bread, soda and canned soup. The conversation that ensued focused on obesity, heart disease and diabetes in minority communities and the connection between racism and the availability of healthy food choices.

Students who have opted to become vegan or vegetarian are only too happy to discuss their reasons for doing so. Frequently, they bring up factory farming and the shocking ways in which animals are raised and slaughtered. As sources, they introduce documentaries such as *Food, Inc.* and bring in video clips showing animals sandwiched into crates where they are confined for life, with no room to stand, let alone move. We get to see cattle being quartered while still alive; disease-ridden chickens that are so fat from hormones that they cannot stand; pigs with their snouts and tails sticking through holes in their crates…

From there the conversation usually takes a turn towards Fast Food and its life-threatening consequences. Many of the students have seen the film, *Super Size Me* (2004), Morgan Spurlock's experiment in eating solely at McDonald's for a month; they are aware that his diet led to drastic physical and psychological side-effects, as well as to weight-gain— 24lbs. in 30 days! Eagerly, they discuss how calories, fat, sugar, preservatives, artificial flavorings and coloring create a potent recipe for chronic illness. Some can even share personal stories regarding their own struggles with fast food related obesity.

There are usually one or two students in the class who will point out that the world's addiction to hamburgers has led to the conversion of the rain forests to grazing land. They will explain how the rain forests are not only essential for stabilizing global climate, but are also home to many species of animals as well as to plants with healing properties. When the trees are toppled, all life within the rain forest either dies or is displaced— as are the indigenous peoples who might live in those regions. In fact, when the human residents oppose the clearing of the forests, they are often killed by loggers...

Gradually, as one topic merges with the next, students are on their smart phones, researching for themselves some aspect of what somebody else has said. Exclamations of shock and horror fill the classroom, not because of my comments but because of their own "finger tip" research. Within minutes, we have touched on racism, animal cruelty, chronic and terminal illness, global farming, the extinction of species, human trafficking, GMO crops, food safety, the need for food labeling and countless other topics.

And the stories keep coming. One student narrates her "near death" experience following an allergic reaction to the pesticides on her bowl of strawberries. Another describes how his brother was diagnosed as having ADHD and was put on medication for years until his symptoms were finally traced to food additives. Several students describe their struggles with eating disorders. Yet another student explains how GMO seed ruined his uncle's farm in Mexico.....

By the end of our first class, students understand that FOOD is a topic that has endless possibilities for research, most of which are directly related to social justice issues. Once students have selected their topics, they become the class experts on that subject and are expected to provide periodic updates about their research. Happily, they are able to maintain their enthusiasm through all the stages of writing until the end of the semester.

At Columbia College, another secular school, I teach courses in spirituality for the Humanities Department; there, too, I incorporate environmental issues into my syllabi. In my course, *Exploring the Goddess*, we study images of the Divine Feminine in multiple cultures through the lenses of archaeology, sociology, psychology, art, mythology, religion and history; we also examine "Mother Earth," equating the ways Earth is treated with the way women are treated across the globe. Mountain top removal, fracking, deforestation, pollution, the generation of toxic waste— all these practices are akin to the disrespect, abuse, rape and control that women experience on a daily basis. Instead of promoting life and technologies of production, humanity deals in death, warping science and technology into what Riane Eisler names as "technologies of destruction" (45). And those who suffer the most tend to be women and children.

Through a variety of assignments, students explore connections between consumerism and poverty, between corporate greed and exploitation, between a "dominator society" (Eisler xvii ff.) and persecution. In one assignment, students work in pairs to create dramatic monologues in which a goddess of their choice rails at some violation of the Earth, lamenting over the atrocities she has witnessed. They then perform their monologues, using props, costumes and audio-visual materials to communicate their message: Artemis, Greek Goddess of the Hunt, grieves over the decimation of forests; Pele, Hawaiian Fire Goddess, spews forth anger in response to mountain surface coal mining; Freya, the great Scandinavian Goddess, cries out against the poisoning of the land; Persephone, daughter of Demeter, wails for all the lost women who have been taken into captivity as sex slaves; Athena, Greek Goddess of Crafts and Wisdom, screams out on behalf of women in the garment industry who are locked into squalid factories for twelve hour shifts without a bathroom break…..

The directions for this assignment are as follows:

> With your study partner, select any goddess from our text and supplement what you have read with stories/artistic representations of this goddess from other sources; both of you should be involved equally in the research and in the creative activity. The more data you have, the fuller your picture of your selected goddess will be. Your task is to create a dramatic monologue in which the goddess cries out against some current social issue. For example, Athena, Goddess of Crafts, may cry out against the conditions women suffer in sweat shops; Artemis, Goddess of the Hunt, may cry out against the extermination of wolves or the slaughter of sharks; Aphrodite, Goddess of Love, may express outrage over human trafficking for sexual purposes etc. Take care to match your goddess to the right issue. Then let the goddess come alive in what you write, making your dramatic monologue as descriptive

and powerful as you possibly can while remaining true to the profile of the goddess.

Try to be as authentic as possible including historical details and appropriate vocabulary and style. Capture the drama and the injustice; let your goddess speak for herself and for women everywhere. You may bring in a brief video clip and/or your research notes to provide background information for your presentation.

The final assignment for this course involves both an integrating essay and an original work of art. Students may work individually or in groups to create either an artistic statement that illustrates the planetary emergency we are facing at the present time, or some sign of hope in response to this emergency. They can use any medium— dance, storytelling, ritual, drama, poetry, music, sculpture, photography, a painting…. The only requirements are 1) absolute originality 2) the work must be presented during the final class in 5-10 minutes.

The essay, on the other hand, outlines their creative process:

> This is a formal writing assignment explaining the genesis of your art project and how it relates to class content. Please show how your final project has been influenced by our texts, discussions and activities; include brief citations from our texts using the MLA format of documentation, as well as references to audio-visual materials and other resources. Also explain why you chose the medium you have worked in, the types of challenges you have faced, and any other information relevant to your creative process. The paper can be written in the first person but is not a journal entry!

I never cease to be amazed at the quality and variety of these projects. Final class is *always* an inspirational experience in which students— mostly majoring in the arts and media— demonstrate what they have learned. Countless projects come to mind: a tiny garden planted in tea cups from a thrift shop; a dress made out of newspapers; a rug woven from plastic shopping bags; an oil painting (later given to me as a gift!) showing the effects of acid rain on the landscape; photographs of a student who, covered in molasses, re-enacts the agony of wild life caught in an oil spill; a dance embodying a woman crushed by patriarchy who ultimately finds her voice; a video of a consumer who eventually lets go of his many possessions, as well as of his debt; a children's picture book showing the importance of recycling; a guide to sustainable living; a kit for roof top gardening; a demonstration on how to prepare a balanced vegetarian meal....

My only regret is that I have never created an archive, let alone an exhibit, of student work. At the same time, however, I am left with the satisfaction that my students have learned for life, not just for a course. Each of them makes some commitment to live more sustainably and to use art as a tool for awakening others to important ecological considerations.

While on the subject of Millennials and sustainable living, I should make note of two topics that really capture their interest. The first has to do with the personal products we use on a daily basis; the second, with products we use around the home. Students are shocked to discover that many name-brand products have harmful ingredients that take their toll on body, mind and environment! *Johnson & Johnson*, a brand that parents have trusted since the 1950's, recently acknowledged that its baby shampoo not only contained *formaldehyde*, a known carcinogen, but also *1.4 dioxane*, a suspected carcinogen. In 2012, the company made a public commitment to remove these and other toxins from its line of baby products, promising at the same time to hold its popular adult products -- *Neutrogena, Aveeno* and *Clean & Clear* – to the same standards by 2015.

Students learn that hair dyes are particularly problematic. Those used by males often have high *lead acetate* content— ten times higher than what is permissible in a can of paint! Because *lead acetate* is known to be a cancer-causing agent, several products American men use to cover their grey hair have been banned in Europe and Canada. Hair coloring used by women is not much better. Though companies eliminated some of the 5,000 chemicals that go into the manufacturing of hair dyes in the 1970's because they caused cancer in lab animals, studies still find a connection between the use of hair colorants and certain types of cancer. Dark hair dyes, for example, have been found to increase the risk of non-Hodgkin's lymphoma and leukemia.

Students discover that there are other harmful ingredients in products such as shampoos, gels, conditioners, hair sprays and setting lotions. *Parabens,* used as preservatives, may extend the shelf life of personal products ranging from shampoos to body lotion, but they mimic estrogen in the way they affect the body and, in some studies, have been linked to breast-cancer, neurological disorders and hormonal problems; though many companies are now marketing *paraben*-free products, *parabens* can still be found in popular products listed under *methyl paraben, ethyl paraben, propyl paraben, butyl paraben, isobutyl paraben* or *E216.*

Coal tar, an ingredient found in dandruff shampoo, is known to cause skin cancer when used in ointments for skin disease; there have also been studies that link industrial exposure to coal tar as a cause of scrotal cancer, lung cancer and urinary bladder cancer. Roofers working with coal tar seem to experience higher risk when it comes to cancers of the oral cavity, larynx, esophagus, stomach, skin and bladder as well as leukemia.

As a result of class discussions, my students become increasingly aware that our use of common personal products comes with a price tag – our health! When we reach for a brand-name deodorant on a supermarket shelf, unless we read the ingredients carefully, we might miss the fact that it most likely contains *aluminum*, a product linked to the epidemic of breast cancer in women. Or when we carelessly place a tube of fluoride toothpaste in our shopping cart, we are oblivious that sodium fluoride is a deadly poison, a key ingredient in Prozac, Sarin Nerve Gas, and rat and roach poison; Hitler, in fact, is reputed to have used fluoride to sterilize humans and numb prisoners into passive submission. *Shocking, yes?* Millennials think so!

I advise my students to read the ingredients of every personal product they happen to use and then to check the safety of those ingredients! (They can do so at http://www.ewg.org/skindeep/). In the supportive environment of the classroom, they learn to make informed choices about personal products and the risks they are willing to take. To their relief, they discover there are healthy alternatives that will not break the bank! Almond oil, for example, works well as eye make-up remover and hair conditioner and can also be used instead of body lotion. Witch hazel (non-alcohol based) can be used as a facial cleanser or astringent. Rose Water makes a wonderful fragrance, while henna provides a natural alternative to hair coloring.

Enthusiastically, my students share with each other brand information regarding lipsticks without lead content, nail polish without formaldehyde, mascara without coal tar, deodorant without aluminum.... They discuss beauty recipes made from kitchen ingredients— oatmeal scrubs utilizing sugar or salt; olive oil and honey moisturizers; cucumber slices to reduce puffiness around the eyes. Though their first reaction to our discussion tends to be one of helpless frustration, they soon move into feeling empowered as they find their own solutions and alternative products.

Our next class topic is to discuss the toxins in household products that can be deadly for our health; many ingredients, in fact, have been linked to serious illnesses and disabilities. Household cleaners, for example, like personal products, are usually chemically based. Simply polishing the wood work or cleaning the silver can lead to neurological damage, while spraying winter boots with a water repellent is even more deadly! Fumes from paint not only cause headaches (unless it is "green" or environmentally safe) but can bring on asthma attacks, sinusitis, dizzy spells and neurological damage; the regular inhaling of paint fumes or the fumes of paint solvents has also been linked to birth defects, infertility and, according to some Danish studies, to a pre-senile condition known as "painter's dementia."

Pesticides used to combat bed bugs in new mattresses, bedding and sofas fumigate us as well as the bugs. Candles designed to create a romantic atmosphere contain lead; they, like chemically-based air fresheners, pollute the very air we breathe. That thick, plush carpet gets it softness from synthetic fibers treated with synthetic chemicals; over time, the carpet emits volatile organic compounds (VOCs) which not only cause headaches and nausea, but can lead to respiratory disease and nerve damage. If the carpet has been treated with fire retardants containing PBDEs, there can be damage to the thyroid and immune system.

By now, however, my students are ready to look for alternatives. They realize that even if they are on a tight budget, there are steps they can take to detoxify their homes. First of all, they can replace chemically-based cleaners with natural products, avoiding anything containing coloring or fragrances. They learn that white vinegar diluted with equal parts of water functions as a natural deodorizer and cleaner. Avoiding marble and granite surfaces which it will stain, this vinegar solution is a power-house when it comes to cleaning bathtubs, toilets, sinks, laminate surfaces, appliances, tile and floors.

They discover that they can also use half a cup of vinegar to replace fabric softener during the laundry rinse cycle. If they or someone they know happens to have a blocked drain, equal parts of baking soda and vinegar, followed by a kettle of boiling water should do the trick. Lemon juice also has its non-culinary uses. Mixed with baking soda, it can be used to scrub dishes and shine brass and copper. Lemon peel freshens garbage disposals and treats stains; mixed with olive oil, it can be used as furniture polish for hardwood furniture. Finally, baking soda also functions as a natural deodorizer— an open box placed in the refrigerator will make all the difference!

Millennials are willing to put in the time and effort to learn more about sustainable living. They appreciate an educational experience that directly relates to their lives; they also enjoy creative activities that measure their grasp of knowledge without subjecting them to quizzes, exams and excessively long research papers. Even if you decide against using *Laudato Si'* as a text, you can introduce some of its specific themes as well as those that represent "the spirit" of the encyclical. It is true that Pope Francis neither mentions personal products nor household cleaning agents, but he does cite John Paul II on the need for "profound changes in lifestyles, models of production and consumption" (#2). Helping young adults make life-giving consumer choices not only encourages them to lead healthier lives but is ultimately healthier for the planet.

CHAPTER SIX

Teaching Generation Z

Today's children were born post 9/11 into an unsafe world. They are used to hearing about violence or seeing it first hand, either on the screen or in their own neighborhoods; they are exposed to news stories that would traumatize the most hardened amongst us and are familiar with the realities of terrorism and climate change. In fact, because they are almost permanently digitally connected, their general knowledge can be quite extraordinary. As in the case of the Millennials, pinpointing exactly when the Z's came on the scene is unclear, but it would seem that the oldest (born pre 9/11) are just entering college while the youngest are still being born.

My own grandson is a Z and he was born in 2005. Only yesterday, he was talking to me about the barbaric policies of North Korea's Kim Jong Un and the global spread of the so called Islamic State. We also had a frank discussion about Trophy Hunting, sparked, of course, by the international outcry over the death of Zimbabwe's Cecil the Lion at the hands of American dentist, Walter Palmer. Ten years old....

This generation is more accustomed to playing video games than going to the park. Today's children outgrow traditional toys very quickly but own the latest technology – iPhones, iPads, game consoles such as Playstation and Xbox. They are more into Esports than real sports and see gaming as a valid sports activity, worthy of Olympic recognition. Esports, by the way, is a multi-million dollar gaming business that has become so popular that there is a growing movement supporting the inclusion of digital athletes at future Olympics! In fact, *Robert Morris University, Chicago*, offers athletic scholarships to gamers and has its own gaming sports team.

(http://www.nytimes.com/2014/12/09/technology/esports-colleges-breeding-grounds-professional-gaming.html?_r=0)

From an early age, Gen Z children have been immersed in the world of *Minecraft, Assassin's Creed,* and *Grand Theft Auto.* Though such games are intended for "mature" teens and adults, many youngsters have easy access to these games and, in fact, find age-appropriate alternatives to be boring. As in the case of Millennials, they are not "readers" but learn from *YouTube* and video games, some of which have detailed historical settings; their outlook tends to be global (because multiplayer games connect them to players from all over the world) and inclusive.

If you teach Generation Z, you will face some of the same academic issues that are true of Millennials— poor reading and writing skills, a need for constant stimulation, the tendency to multi-task, an inability to sit still .... Just as Gen X was raised on *Sesame Street*, so Gen Z is being raised on smart phones and MacAir laptops.

Surprisingly independent, Gen Z children are hungry for attention, but may not even know it. Raised by parents who are themselves digitally distracted, many Gen Z kids experience more solitary "screen time" than personal interaction with one or both parents. Visit any park, observe families eating in restaurants or simply watch a mother pushing a stroller— what you will find is that the adults in charge are either texting or on *Facebook* while supposedly enjoying "quality time" with their offspring. Worse still, it is not uncommon to see children as young as three and four years of age amusing themselves on iPhones while their parents are preoccupied. The smart phone has become a babysitter and Gen Z's ideas and values are shaped by social media rather than family values.

Like Millennials, Gen Z children feel at a loss without digital connection. Losing an iPhone or having it become temporarily unavailable brings on an existential crisis; their identity, sense of security, relationships and, in fact, their whole world depend on a "thing" that can fit in the palm of their hands— and that's where it usually is. Some, in spite of all the medical data suggesting that this is ***not*** a good idea, even sleep with their smart phones under their pillows!

Given all the above, if you can introduce the children in your classroom to a few of the concepts underlying ***Laudato Si'***, you are not only promoting sustainable living but also exposing your students to a world beyond the iPhone. In fact, you have a unique opportunity to assist in the spiritual formation of your charges, even in settings where religion is unwelcome. This is especially true for those of you who may teach pre-school or primary grades. Now, of course, you have a curriculum to follow and, if you teach in the public school system, there is the additional burden of ongoing testing and assessment. In spite of these limitations, however, it is still possible to make space for an ecological agenda.

Let's begin with pre-school. Young children are natural contemplatives, filled with wonder and amazement over the workings of Nature. If you are fortunate enough to be working with a pre-digitalized group of children, your task is easy. Early on in the encyclical, Pope Francis writes: *"Rather than a problem to be solved, the world is a joyful mystery to be contemplated with gladness and praise"* (#12). The key terms here are:

1. World= joyful mystery

2. Contemplated

3. Gladness

4. Praise

In a religious school, all four terms can become the basis of classroom activity; in a secular setting, the first three terms can easily become a focus.

Cultivating a sense of joy and wonder in your students can become part of your mission. There is no need to put this in writing or to articulate it to anyone; what is important is that you, yourself, consciously undertake to promote these values. Decades ago, when I first began teaching

Composition in university settings, I made it my unspoken/unwritten agenda to awaken my students to "isms" such as sexism, racism, anti-Semitism and homophobia. Over the years, my "mission" grew to include other forms of social injustice, both global and local. My agenda does not appear on my syllabi, nor has it ever been approved by a department chair. Rather, I intentionally select readings, design assignments, plan field trips, bring in guest speakers and lead class discussions to communicate values I hold dear. Am I guilty of brainwashing? I hope not. Rather, I use my place of privilege as instructor to present new ideas which my students are free to accept or reject.

Back to your pre-schoolers! What classroom activities can support joy and wonder? What can you grow, observe and care for? Perhaps you already have a list of successful strategies that have worked for your students in the past; or perhaps you can still remember activities that excited you when you were little. I think back to my early years of schooling and to some of the more memorable activities that have left an impact on me: watching tadpoles morph into frogs; growing beans in jam jars and observing roots and shoots begin to form; caring for a sickly baby hedgehog; planting sun flower seeds and marigold seeds; collecting brilliantly-colored leaves in the fall; gathering acorns and sycamore seeds; cracking the prickly exteriors of horse chestnut seed capsules to release the shiny "conkers" within….

Those were days of innocence and delight, when the world was truly green and I was "green and carefree," like the subject of Dylan Thomas' poem, *Fern Hill*, excerpted below:

And as I was green and carefree, famous among
the barns
About the happy yard and singing as the farm
was home,
In the sun that is young once only,
Time let me play and be
Golden in the mercy of his means
And green and golden I was huntsman and
herdsman, the calves

Sang to my horn, the foxes on the hill barked
clear and cold,
And the Sabbath rang slowly
In the pebbles of the holy streams.

If your pre-schoolers are still "green and carefree," there are so many ways you can teach them to love and respect Nature. A reading of Shel Silverstein's *The Giving Tree* can awaken a sense of gratitude for trees which do so much for all of us— providing shelter and shade, giving us clean air, regulating the flow of storm waters, calming frayed nerves, creating a habitat for countless creatures.... This wonderful book awakens compassion in the readers or listeners who come to understand that some trees give everything —their bark, their limbs, their trunks— that we may have furniture, and swing sets and paper.

Following a simple discussion, the class can go outside to an area where the children can each hug a tree and thank it for its generosity. Perhaps the children can even make eco-friendly gifts to decorate a favorite tree or write poems (with assistance!) about a tree that they know and love. A child who has connected with trees at a very young age is less likely to carve graffiti in bark, to tear off leaves and break off branches; that same child may be more conscious about the use of paper and the need to conserve furniture and other articles made from wood.

Another activity could be celebrating the children's pets or a pet they know and love that belongs to someone else. They could bring in photos of their pets or else draw pictures of them in class. They would then introduce their classmates to their pet, explaining what they love the most about it and what makes it special. After that, they could create stories— or puppet shows— with their cat, dog or budgie as the hero. Helping small children understand that pets can experience physical and emotional pain encourages them to be kind and protective towards animals— more responsible, more attentive and less rough.

Creating a Nature Table in the classroom, with each child contributing some treasure, would be another way of awakening wonder and gratitude. Seeds, sea shells, fossils, feathers, birds' nests (empty, of course!), flowers— each item becomes an object of wonder, a means of exploring the diversity and beauty of the Earth we call home. In a religious school, children can gather around the table for a simple prayer of gratitude:

Dear God, we thank you for...

To this day, I still remember the refrain from a hymn I learned in kindergarten at my Protestant Day School in England; because this is a resource that you may wish to use in your class, the entire hymn follows:

Refrain:
All things bright and beautiful,
all creatures great and small,
all things wise and wonderful:
the Lord God made them all.

1. Each little flower that opens,
each little bird that sings,

God made their glowing colors,
and made their tiny wings.
(Refrain)

2. The purple-headed mountains,
the river running by,
the sunset and the morning
that brightens up the sky.
(Refrain)

3. The cold wind in the winter,
the pleasant summer sun,
the ripe fruits in the garden:
God made them every one.
(Refrain)

4. God gave us eyes to see them,
and lips that we might tell
how great is God Almighty,
who has made all things well.
(Refrain)

The bottom line— whether in a secular
school or religious school— is to let your
classroom become a true "kindergarten,"
that is, a place where youngsters will be

nurtured like the flowers in a garden. That was the original idea of German educator, Friedrich Frobel (1782–1852), who re-named his play and activity institute for children *Kindergarten* on June 28, 1840. Interestingly enough, gardening was one of the activities he promoted for young children, along with singing, dancing and building blocks.

(https://en.wikipedia.org/wiki/Kindergarten)

"But what of older children?" you might ask. "What happens if I am working with children who have left Disney and Santa Claus behind and who are obsessed with video games? What happens if the kids I teach are already cynical, "tuned out" and engrossed in a *virtual* world instead of the *real* world? How can I instill a sense of awe and wonder in these children while encouraging them to be good stewards of creation?"

In such a situation, the challenge is going to be formidable but not impossible. In the first place, I would suggest using technology to reach your students. Teach them the art of "contemplative photography" whereby instead of simply taking *selfies* and snap shots, they begin to use their phone cameras to record the unfurling of a leaf, the opening of a bud, the hatching of an egg, the sprouting of a seed. Even if they are not permitted to bring their phones to school, you can give them a class on "seeing" (as opposed to "glancing") and then ask them to take photographs outside school as an assignment. Their task might be to explore the natural world and to record what they find: perhaps a spider weaving a web or a bee gathering pollen; perhaps a squirrel gathering acorns or a baby rabbit nibbling the Impatiens; perhaps a duck swimming with her young or geese flying overhead....

What is important is that the students SEE the world around them. Instead of walking, heads bent, focusing on their smart phones, they can become aware of the incredible beauty that is only visible to those who take the time to observe.

Of course, the students will need to a way to share their photos. Prints may be impractical but setting up a class *Facebook* page that focuses on "Mother Earth" could be a solution. Regardless of the format you choose for sharing, always focus on the purpose behind the assignment— learning to "behold" Nature. Which students have spent the most time in observation? Who has captured the most amazing moment? What can each student share with his or her classmates about their experience of "seeing"?

Secondly, I would engage the students creatively. Perhaps they could invent a board game on *Saving Mother Earth* as a prototype for a videogame; this type of assignment would definitely engage their interest while reinforcing such skills as research, art and creative writing. The "video game assignment" would also involve a discussion, adapted to the maturity-level of the students, about some of the real issues facing the planet. Although Gen Z children are used to violence on the screen, for all their bravado they are likely to be terrified at the thought of impending catastrophe. The information provided therefore needs to be clear, simple and non-threatening. For children in primary grades, for example, the focus could be on 1) recycling 2) not littering 3) conserving water 4) avoiding waste 5) sharing with others 6) being kind to animals.

Older children may be ready to study global warming but always as a problem that can be solved, not as a force that is going to destroy the world. They may be ready to examine their own carbon foot print and to consider ways they might live more sustainably. The focus would be on finding every day solutions that they themselves can implement.

Another assignment—perhaps for Junior High— would be to have students work in small group to compose the lyrics to a "rap song" on saving the Earth. Creating art from trash that they themselves have collected would be another possibility; they could also design eco-friendly fashions or housing solutions. One project that I have found successful at the college level would also work here, but with some "sanitary guidelines" attached: students analyze the trash their family generates in a single day (or week) and then evaluate how their family could live more sustainably, according to the 3 R's— Reduce, Recycle, Re-use.

With thought and careful planning, any class for students of any age can reflect the spirit and intentions behind *Laudato Si'*. You, as the teacher, will best know what might work for your particular group of students, in your particular socio-economic, geographic area. Again, the purpose of introducing eco-spirituality to children is not to teach them "facts" or to terrify them with what *might* happen, but to awaken them to the wondrous universe which is their inheritance. With that goal in mind, you will discover endless pedagogical activities that will engage the minds and hearts of those in your care, while providing you, their teacher, with a renewed sense of mission and, perhaps, a greener perspective!

THE GARDEN

There is a garden
in my mind—
fertile triangle enclosed
by ancient limestone walls
massive as fortifications
built against Turkish onslaught
in centuries past.
Across the glass shards
which guard these walls,
ivy geraniums curl tendrils,
spill pink blossoms
out, over
to the dusty roadside,
startling passers-by
with sudden hue
and unexpected fragrance.

Inside,
bougainvillea creeps purple;
the poinsettia splashes red
ten feet high,
weaving rich tapestry
across white stone,
fitting backdrop

for celosia, zinnias
and nasturtiums,
for citrus trees
and flowering shrubs.

The vines are heavy
with grapes
and, sticky with sweet ooze,
the St. John's fig
yields its second crop.

Ants assault the split skins
of fallen fruit, keeping fellowship
with somnolent wasps,
drunk with fermenting feast
on hot summer days.
Snakes slither
along sun-baked earth
while in and out of crannies
salamanders dart
sleek and shining,
too quick for Angelu's hoe
as he weeds, breaks clumps,
cuts back foliage...

On the terrace,
tea is served—

ritual of cucumber sandwiches,
scones, McVities Biscuits,
milk for the children.
Grandpa sits straight and lean,
surveying flowerbeds
ablaze with color,
well-content
with the display
as he cradles china cup
in aging hands.

Later, in the cool
of early evening,
I skip down garden paths,
wary of the roses,
stop to watch the goldfish,
then take my turn
on the swing,
working fat legs
until I can see
high, high over the walls—
terraced fields, flat roofs,
and far beyond, a thin line
of Mediterranean blue…

Now the images fade,
leaving only wilderness,
brown, brittle, unwatered;
now, with shovels raised,
bulldozers wait
to begin the wrecking.

Elizabeth-Anne Stewart, *Extraordinary Time*.

WORKS CITED

Bonaventure. *The Soul's Journey into God.* NJ: Paulist Press, 1978.

Boyce, J.K. *Economics, the Environment and Our Common Wealth.* MA: Edward Elgar, 2013.

Campbell, Joseph. *The Power of Myth.* NY: Doubleday, 1988.

Eisler, Riane. *The Chalice and the Blade.* NY: HarperCollins, 1987.

Kenner, Robert. *Food, Inc.* (movie). 2010.

Hawken, Paul. *Blessed Unrest.* NY: Penguin Books, 2007.

Hoffman, Edward. *The Heavenly Ladder.* NY: Four Worlds Press, 1985.

http://www.catholicworldreport.com/Item/3 960/laudato_si_focuses_on_the_heart_of_m an_and_the_disorders_of_our_age.aspx

http://www.ewg.org/skindeep/

http://kids.sandiegozoo.org/animals/insects/dung-beetle

http://www.motherjones.com/blue-marble/2015/06/dear-rick-santorum-pope-actually-did-study-science

http://www.ncbi.nlm.nih.gov/pubmed/21233435

http://www.newsweek.com/jeb-bush-pope-youre-not-boss-me-343922

http://www.nytimes.com/2014/12/09/technology/esports-colleges-breeding-grounds-professional-gaming.html?_r=0

http://remnantnewspaper.com/web/index.php/fetzen-fliegen/item/1819-why-i-m-disregarding-laudato-si-and-you-should-too

http://reshafim.org.il/ad/egypt/negative_confessions/index.html

https://en.wikipedia.org/wiki/Kindergarten

Parliament of the World's Religions. *The Global Ethic*. Chicago, IL: PWR, 1993.

Patricca, Nicholas. *The Fifth Sun*. IL; Dramatic Publishing Co, 1986.

Silverstein, Shel. *The Giving Tree*. NY: HarperCollins, 1999.

Spurlock, Morgan, *Super Size Me* (movie), 2004.

Thomas, Dylan. "Fern Hill." http://www.poemhunter.com/poem/fern-hill/

Vanek (Stewart), Elizabeth-Anne. *Extraordinary Time. OH: Daring Books, 1988.*

Vanek (Stewart), Elizabeth-Anne. *Woman Dreamer*. Bristol, IN: Wyndham Hall Press, 1989.

ABOUT THE AUTHOR

Born in England and raised both in England and on the tiny Mediterranean island of Malta, **Elizabeth-Anne Stewart** is a life-long spiritual seeker who guides others through her preaching, teaching, spiritual direction, life coaching and writings. Though she lives in Chicago, Malta has always been her "sacred landscape," the setting for much of her poetry and prose as well as a place of pilgrimage to which she has brought many groups of American students, mostly from DePaul University where she taught and ministered for twenty-eight years.

She earned a PhD in Theology from the University of Malta, as well as a B.A. in English, but holds several other degrees and certificates from British and American institutions. The author of *Sunday BibleTalk*, a monthly online scripture service based on Sunday's liturgical readings, she offers retreats and workshops across the U.S. and internationally.

More information about Dr. Stewart's many books and articles can be found at
www.elizabethannestewart.com

CPSIA information can be obtained at www.ICGtesting.com
Printed in the USA
BVOW02s2326040915

416737BV00001B/9/P